BUSY·LITTLE·HANDS

PAPER
MODELS THAT WORK

A FIRST CRAFT BOOK FOR PARENT AND CHILD

Illustrated by
DOUGLAS HALL

HAMLYN

Introduction

It's always fun to try out something new – so why not make a paper model! Once you have learned the basic methods required and with a little skill, you will be surprised how easy it is to make an effective model.

Like all crafts, modelling in paper needs patience and practise. Your first efforts may be a bit disappointing, but don't be put off – keep trying and you will soon see an improvement in your ability.

You won't need to collect a lot of equipment to make paper models, but a list of items appears on page 6.

An ideal paper to use for models is *cartridge paper.* This is often used for drawing or writing: it is quite stiff, yet thin enough to cut and fold easily. Plain white cartridge can be easily painted, but it can also be purchased in a ready-made range of colours.

Carton board is better for models that require a thicker and stiffer material. This is also quite easy to cut, but it should be scored before it is folded (see page 6). Carton board is used to make cornflake and soap boxes, so when these are empty, save them for your models.

Look out for odd scraps of spare paper and card – coloured, textured or patterned – you never know when they might be useful for a particular model. If you have difficulty finding exactly what you need for a model, you will find that all types of paper and card can be bought from a good art shop.

Wherever possible the plans in this book are drawn actual size, but a few are drawn to a reduced scale. Where this occurs measurements are given for guidance. Details have been added to trace and colour.

I hope you enjoy making the items in this book – and have lots of fun making paper models of your own.

...but do remember!

★ Scissors, especially pointed ones, are dangerous if they are left open. Always keep them closed when you are not using them.

★ Paper can give you a nasty cut, especially if you run your finger along its edge too quickly – so don't rush!

★ Before using glue of any sort on a tabletop, lay a sheet of plastic cloth or a newspaper over your work area. Never use too much glue!

★ Finally, keep your hands clean – and be sure to tidy away all your paper cuttings when you have finished your model.

Contents

Starting Off

Let's begin by looking at the tools and equipment you will need for making paper models. First of all, you will need a sharp pair of scissors – pointed ones are useful for snipping out tiny details.

You will need some tracing paper for tracing the designs and some carbon paper for transferring the design to your model paper or card. (Use old carbon paper as it is not so black as new carbon.)

For thicker card you will need a scoring point, but if you don't have one, you can use an old small-size knitting needle. Make sure the point is not too sharp or you will cut right through the card instead of scoring it.

If you have a compass for drawing circles, so much the better, but if not you can draw a circle by using the method shown on the opposite page.

Any type of glue that is quick drying, like *balsa cement*, is ideal for paper models. *Resin-W* is also very good, and stronger, but it takes a little longer to dry. Double-sided adhesive tape is sometimes quicker to use for some jobs than glue – and it's not so messy!

Keep all your tools in a good strong cardboard box – keep them tidy and have fun!

Your Papercraft Kit

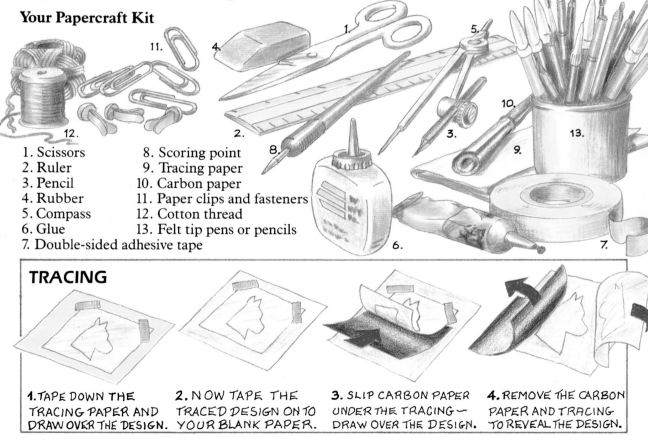

1. Scissors
2. Ruler
3. Pencil
4. Rubber
5. Compass
6. Glue
7. Double-sided adhesive tape
8. Scoring point
9. Tracing paper
10. Carbon paper
11. Paper clips and fasteners
12. Cotton thread
13. Felt tip pens or pencils

TRACING

1. TAPE DOWN THE TRACING PAPER AND DRAW OVER THE DESIGN.

2. NOW TAPE THE TRACED DESIGN ON TO YOUR BLANK PAPER.

3. SLIP CARBON PAPER UNDER THE TRACING – DRAW OVER THE DESIGN.

4. REMOVE THE CARBON PAPER AND TRACING TO REVEAL THE DESIGN.

SCORING AND FOLDING

1. FOLDING THIN PAPER IS EASY ~ FOLD OVER ALONG THE FOLD LINE AND PRESS FLAT.

2. THICKER PAPER OR CARD WILL NEED SCORING BEFORE IT IS FOLDED.

3. HOLD YOUR RULER FIRMLY DOWN ON THE FOLD LINE.

4. RUN THE SCORING POINT FIRMLY ALONG THE EDGE OF THE RULER.

...NOW YOU CAN FOLD.

GLUING

1. ALWAYS APPLY GLUE TO ONE SURFACE ONLY ~ APPLY SPARINGLY.

2. REMEMBER THAT THE GLUE WILL SPREAD OUT WHEN THE TWO PARTS ARE SQUEEZED TOGETHER.

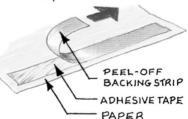

PEEL-OFF BACKING STRIP
ADHESIVE TAPE
PAPER

USING DOUBLE-SIDED ADHESIVE TAPE
1. POSITION TAPE ON PAPER
2. PEEL OFF THE BACKING TO REVEAL THE STICKY TAPE.

ROLLING AND CURLING

2. PULL THE PAPER SLOWLY OUT AND UP FROM UNDER THE RULER, HOLDING IT DOWN FIRMLY AT THE SAME TIME.

1. PLACE THE PAPER BENEATH A HARD EDGE, LIKE A RULER.

DRAWING CIRCLES

THIS IS A SIMPLE WAY TO DRAW A CIRCLE WITHOUT USING A COMPASS. THE DISTANCE HALF-WAY ACROSS A CIRCLE IS CALLED A **RADIUS**.

CENTRE PIN   PENCIL NOTCH
RADIUS DISTANCE

1. BEGIN BY MAKING A COMPASS BEAM FROM SCRAP CARD ~ USE A DRAWING PIN FOR A CENTRE POINT. PUSH IT THROUGH THE CARD.

2. MEASURE THE RADIUS OF YOUR CIRCLE, FROM THE CENTRE PIN, AND THEN CUT A NOTCH IN THE CARD EDGE.

3. USE THE PIN AS YOUR CENTRE ~ PLACE A PENCIL IN THE NOTCH AND PUSH THE BEAM ROUND TO COMPLETE THE CIRCLE.

KEY TO DRAWINGS

ON ALL THE DESIGNS IN THIS BOOK YOU WILL FIND THE LINES ARE DRAWN LIKE THIS:~

CUT LINES
FOLD LINES
DETAIL LINES [Colouring]
TABS [To be glued]

Begin with a Square

Let's begin by making a very simple model from a plain square of paper. It can be any size you like, but remember that the smaller the piece of paper, the harder it is to fold. Follow the drawings carefully, folding as you go from step 1 to step 6.

You will need: 1 piece of paper (not too flimsy) 20cm × 20cm (8in × 8in) square.

Paper Dart

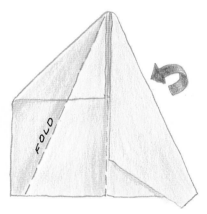

1. BEGIN BY FOLDING THE SQUARE OF PAPER DOWN THE MIDDLE — PRESS FLAT.

2. OPEN OUT THE FOLDED SQUARE AND FOLD IN THE TOP CORNERS TO THE CENTRE.

3. NOW MAKE A SECOND FOLD, TAKING EACH EDGE INTO THE CENTRE FOLD.

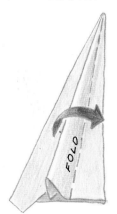

YOU CAN COLOUR YOUR PAPER DART, IF YOU LIKE, TO MAKE IT LOOK REALLY SMART

4. CLOSE UP THE CENTRE FOLD. PRESS FLAT AND THEN FOLD EACH SIDE OUT TO THE OUTER EDGE.

5. WITH BOTH SIDES FOLDED BACK NEATLY, PRESS DOWN FIRMLY TO SHARPEN UP ALL THE CREASES.

6. FINALLY, OPEN OUT THE FLAPS TO MAKE THE WINGS AT EACH SIDE. NOW THE DART WILL FLY!

More Fun with Squares

There are many things that can be made with a simple square of paper. Here, and on the following two pages are some more ideas with squares. Once again, you can make these from any size of paper square, but start off with a 20cm × 20cm (8in × 8in) piece of paper.

Paper Boat

4....AND THEN THE OTHER.

1. BEGIN BY FOLDING THE TOP CORNER TO THE BOTTOM CORNER.

5. OPEN OUT AT THE BASE AND THEN PRESS FLAT...

...LIKE THIS.

2. FOLD IN BOTH THE OUTER POINTS TO THE BOTTOM POINT.

REPEAT STEPS **3** AND **4**.

3. NOW FOLD THE BOTTOM POINTS BACK UP TO THE TOP, ...FIRST ON ONE SIDE...

6. HOLD THE TWO TOP POINTS AND PULL THEM GENTLY AWAY FROM EACH OTHER...

...LIKE THIS. PRESS THE BOAT FLAT.

7. FINALLY, PUSH YOUR FINGERS INSIDE THE BOAT TO PINCH THE SAIL UP INTO SHAPE.

10

Party Hat ...and you can add a feather!

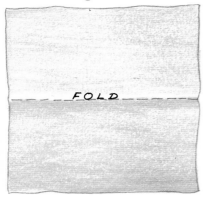

1. BEGIN BY FOLDING THE SQUARE OF PAPER NEATLY IN HALF.

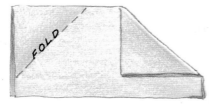

2. FOLD IN BOTH CORNERS, BUT NOT RIGHT TO THE EDGE — ABOUT 2·5cm (1in) FROM THE BOTTOM EDGE.

3. FOLD UP BOTH OF THE BOTTOM EDGES AND PRESS THEM DOWN FLAT.

4. OPEN OUT THE HAT AND TURN UP ONE END — IT DOESN'T MATTER WHICH END.

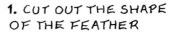

5. PRESS THE HAT FLAT. CUT THE FEATHER SLOTS.

TO MAKE A FEATHER

1. CUT OUT THE SHAPE OF THE FEATHER

2. MAKE ANGLED CUTS DOWN EACH SIDE.

3. FOLD ALONG THE STEM FOR A LITTLE WAY.

4. FINALLY, CURL OVER THE FEATHER EDGES AND PUSH IT INTO THE HAT SLOTS.

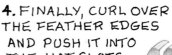

11

Funny Fortunes ★

Here's a great game that will amuse and amaze your friends. Follow the instructions and you will soon become an expert fortune-teller.

You will need: 1 piece of paper 20cm × 20cm (8in × 8in); a pen; some coloured pens or pencils.

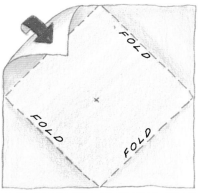

1. BEGIN BY TURNING EACH OF THE FOUR CORNERS INTO THE CENTRE.

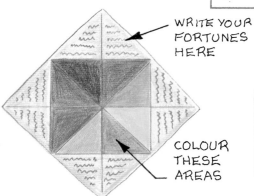

WRITE YOUR FORTUNES HERE

COLOUR THESE AREAS

2. TURN OVER TO THE SMOOTH SIDE AND DIVIDE SQUARE WITH PENCIL LINES AS SHOWN.

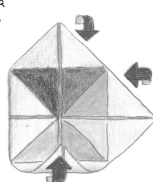

3. NOW, ONCE AGAIN, FOLD EACH OF THE FOUR CORNERS INTO THE CENTRE.

4. NUMBER EACH OF THE SEGMENTS AS SHOWN.

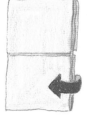

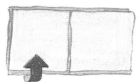

5. FOLD OVER TO COVER THE NUMBERS — FIRST ONE WAY...

...AND THEN THE OTHER.

6. FOLD AGAIN FROM CORNER TO CORNER — FIRST ONE WAY...

...AND THEN THE OTHER.

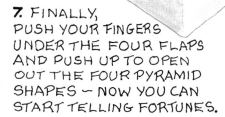

7. FINALLY, PUSH YOUR FINGERS UNDER THE FOUR FLAPS AND PUSH UP TO OPEN OUT THE FOUR PYRAMID SHAPES — NOW YOU CAN START TELLING FORTUNES.

HERE'S WHAT YOU HAVE TO DO

Pinch the four pyramid points together with your fingers and ask a friend to choose a number from 1 to 8. They might, for example, choose number 5. Open up the pyramids and lift flap number 5 — this will reveal the fortune.

THIS IS WHAT YOU SAY

As you reveal the fortune read off what is written on the flap: 'You are...

LUCKY – UNLUCKY – RICH – POOR – YOUR FAVOURITE COLOUR IS – YOU ARE FAT – THIN – YOU'RE GOING TO BE KISSED BY...A GIRL...A BOY...make up your own fortunes and have fun!

Whirly Windmill

Although you can make this whirly windmill with paper, it looks really great if you make it with a piece of coloured acrylic film (you can buy this at an art shop). This is a bit like plastic but it is just as easy to cut as paper and it does not crease.

You will need: 1 piece of coloured paper (or acrylic film) 15cm × 15cm (6in × 6in); 1 thin garden stick about 30cm (12in) long; 1 short length of stiff wire; 2 small beads (the hole in each must be large enough for the wire to pass through easily); and some glue.

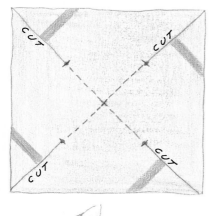

1. START BY DIVIDING THE SQUARE INTO FOUR SEGMENTS.

2. MARK A POINT ON EACH LINE HALF WAY BETWEEN THE CORNERS AND CENTRE.

3. USING SCISSORS, CUT FROM EACH CORNER TO EACH OF THESE HALF-WAY POINTS.

4. CURL UP FOUR OF THE CORNERS, AS SHOWN, AND GLUE THEM ONE AT A TIME IN THE CENTRE. ALL THE POINTS SHOULD OVERLAP.

5. NOW TWIST THE WIRE LIKE THIS.

6. THREAD A BEAD ON TO THE WIRE AND PUSH IT THROUGH THE FOUR OVER-LAPPING POINTS AT THE CENTRE.

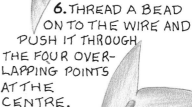

7. FINALLY, THREAD ON A SECOND BEAD AND TWIST THE WIRE SECURELY ROUND THE END OF THE STICK.

13

Triangle Snapper

This is a traditional 'Crackerjack' and it is very easy to make. When you flick the triangle down hard it cracks like a firework. Use coloured card if you can.

You will need: 1 piece of stiff card 20cm (8in) square; 1 piece of thin, but strong, paper 20cm (8in) square; and some glue.

PAPER (CUT 1)

FOLD   FOLD   FOLD

CARD (CUT 1)

FOLD

1. CUT OUT THE TWO MAIN PIECES FOR THE SNAPPER. IF YOU USE COLOURED CARD THE SNAPPER WILL LOOK BRIGHT AND CHEERFUL.

2. FOLD THE PAPER IN HALF AND FOLD BACK THE TWO LONG FLAPS. ▷

3. OPEN OUT AND FOLD ON THE SAME LINES, BUT THE OTHER WAY. ▷

◁ **4.** SCORE AND FOLD THE CARD. GLUE ONE OF THE PAPER FLAPS ALONG THE TOP EDGE OF THE CARD.

5. WHEN THE GLUE IS DRY, STICK THE SECOND FLAP IN PLACE.

6. TUCK THE PAPER INSIDE THE FOLDED CARD AND PRESS FLAT.

14

I ONLY WANT TO SHOW YOU HOW EASY IT IS TO MAKE A TRIANGLE SNAPPER!

CRACK!

7. TO MAKE THE SNAPPER WORK, HOLD IT BY THE BOTTOM CORNER WITH THE PAPER AT THE TOP. FLICK IT DOWN HARD AND THE PAPER WILL SNAP OUT –'CRACK'!

Kazoo

This is the simplest way in the world to be a pop star!

FOLD

ALL YOU NEED IS A PIECE OF TISSUE PAPER...

...AND A COMB.

FOLD THE PAPER OVER THE COMB, PLACE IT TO YOUR LIPS...

...AND HUM!

15

Stick Puppet ★

Although it has lots of pieces, this stick puppet is easy to put together. Once you've succeeded in making one puppet, you can go on to make others, like the characters at the bottom of page 17. You can even create your own puppet theatre.

You will need: 1 piece of stiff card 15cm × 13cm (6in × 5in); 1 thin garden stick about 30cm (12in) long; 6 small paper fasteners; cotton thread; and some glue.

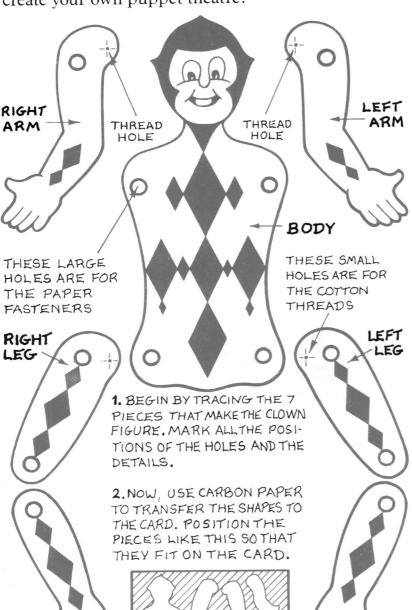

RIGHT ARM

THREAD HOLE

THREAD HOLE

LEFT ARM

BODY

THESE LARGE HOLES ARE FOR THE PAPER FASTENERS

THESE SMALL HOLES ARE FOR THE COTTON THREADS

RIGHT LEG

LEFT LEG

1. BEGIN BY TRACING THE 7 PIECES THAT MAKE THE CLOWN FIGURE. MARK ALL THE POSITIONS OF THE HOLES AND THE DETAILS.

2. NOW, USE CARBON PAPER TO TRANSFER THE SHAPES TO THE CARD. POSITION THE PIECES LIKE THIS SO THAT THEY FIT ON THE CARD.

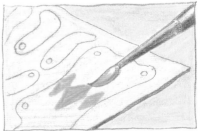

3. IT WILL BE MUCH EASIER TO COLOUR IN THE CLOWN BEFORE YOU START TO CUT OUT ALL THE PIECES.

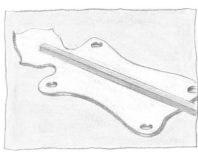

4. CUT OUT THE PIECES AND LAY THE BODY SHAPE FACE DOWN. PLACE THE STICK DOWN THE CENTRE AND...

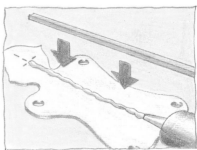

5. ... MARK ITS POSITION. APPLY SOME GLUE DOWN THE BACK OF THE BODY AND FIX THE STICK—LEAVE TO DRY.

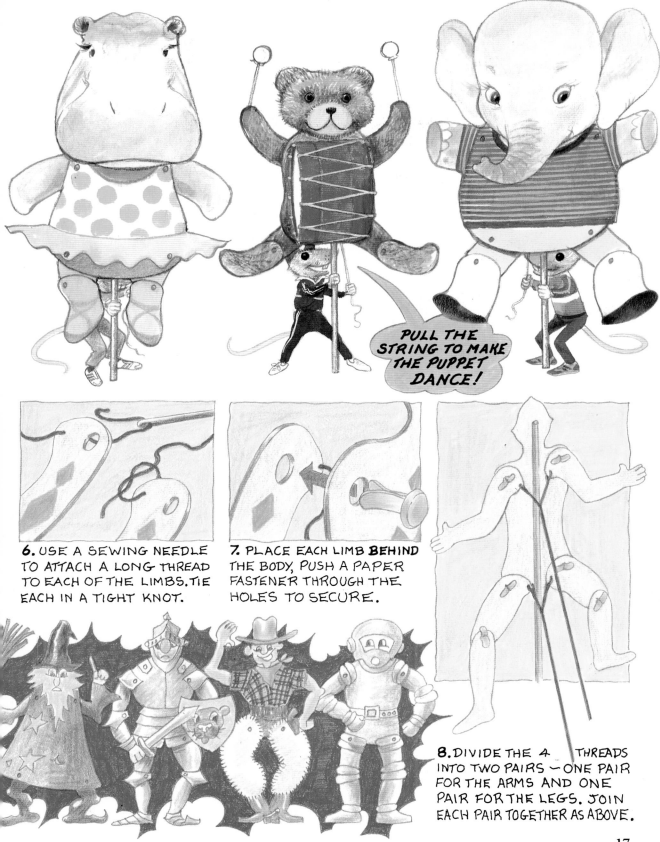

PULL THE STRING TO MAKE THE PUPPET DANCE!

6. USE A SEWING NEEDLE TO ATTACH A LONG THREAD TO EACH OF THE LIMBS. TIE EACH IN A TIGHT KNOT.

7. PLACE EACH LIMB **BEHIND** THE BODY, PUSH A PAPER FASTENER THROUGH THE HOLES TO SECURE.

8. DIVIDE THE 4 THREADS INTO TWO PAIRS — ONE PAIR FOR THE ARMS AND ONE PAIR FOR THE LEGS. JOIN EACH PAIR TOGETHER AS ABOVE.

17

Diamond Kite ★

There's nothing better than flying a kite in a strong summer breeze! This one is not only easy to make but a real high-flyer! Use the size recommended: if you make it smaller it will be hard to control, if you make it bigger you may well fly up with it!

You will need: 1 garden stick 60cm (24in) long; 1 garden stick 40cm (16in) long; 1 large sheet of brown wrapping paper 70cm × 50cm (28in × 20in); some strong thin string; a flying line (cotton or nylon fishing line is best); crepe paper (for the tail); adhesive tape and some glue.

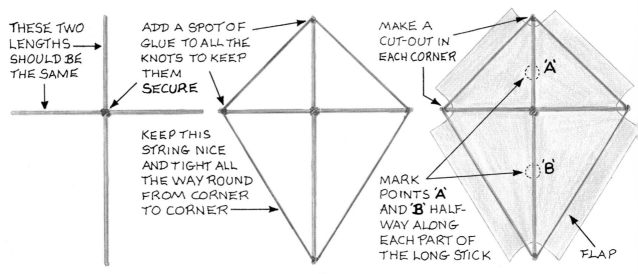

THESE TWO LENGTHS SHOULD BE THE SAME

ADD A SPOT OF GLUE TO ALL THE KNOTS TO KEEP THEM SECURE

KEEP THIS STRING NICE AND TIGHT ALL THE WAY ROUND FROM CORNER TO CORNER

MAKE A CUT-OUT IN EACH CORNER

MARK POINTS 'A' AND 'B' HALF-WAY ALONG EACH PART OF THE LONG STICK

FLAP

1. BEGIN BY PLACING THE STICKS TOGETHER AS SHOWN ABOVE. TIE THEM TOGETHER TIGHTLY.

2. TIE STRONG STRING ALL ROUND – KEEP THE STICKS AT RIGHT ANGLES TO EACH OTHER.

3. LAY THE KITE FRAME ON THE PAPER AND DRAW ROUND IT ALLOWING AT LEAST 5cm (2in) FOR FLAPS.

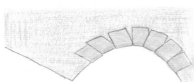

4. STRENGTHEN THE FOUR CORNER CUT-OUTS WITH ADHESIVE TAPE.

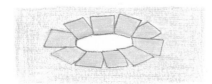

5. CUT TWO HOLES AT 'A' AND 'B' AND STRENGTHEN WITH ADHESIVE TAPE AS ABOVE.

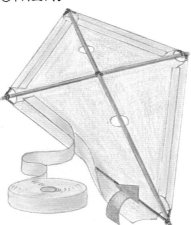

6. PLACE THE FRAME ON THE PAPER, FOLD THE FLAPS OVER THE STRING AND GLUE THEM DOWN. TAPE THE JOINED EDGE.

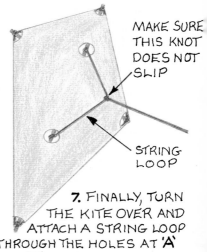

MAKE SURE THIS KNOT DOES NOT SLIP

STRING LOOP

7. FINALLY, TURN THE KITE OVER AND ATTACH A STRING LOOP THROUGH THE HOLES AT 'A' AND 'B'. TIE THE FLYING LINE SECURELY TO THE LOOP.

18

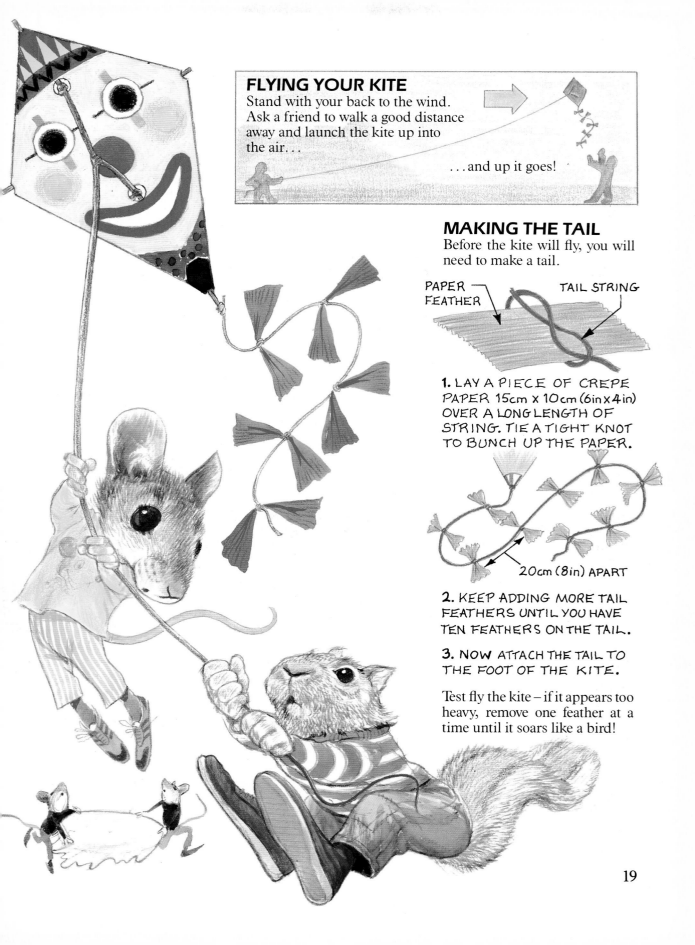

FLYING YOUR KITE

Stand with your back to the wind. Ask a friend to walk a good distance away and launch the kite up into the air...

...and up it goes!

MAKING THE TAIL

Before the kite will fly, you will need to make a tail.

PAPER FEATHER

TAIL STRING

1. LAY A PIECE OF CREPE PAPER 15cm x 10cm (6in x 4in) OVER A LONG LENGTH OF STRING. TIE A TIGHT KNOT TO BUNCH UP THE PAPER.

20cm (8in) APART

2. KEEP ADDING MORE TAIL FEATHERS UNTIL YOU HAVE TEN FEATHERS ON THE TAIL.

3. NOW ATTACH THE TAIL TO THE FOOT OF THE KITE.

Test fly the kite – if it appears too heavy, remove one feather at a time until it soars like a bird!

19

Animal Skittles

You will need: stiff paper or card (the size doesn't really matter); coloured pencils; 1 marble or large round bead; and some glue.

This is a great game to play when you've got nothing to do. Follow the instructions carefully to make the ramp and the animals and you will have a game that can be played by up to four people. You will need to make six animals for the game.

MAKING THE ANIMALS

Let's start off by making a dog.

This is an easy animal to make, but there are lots of others over the page.

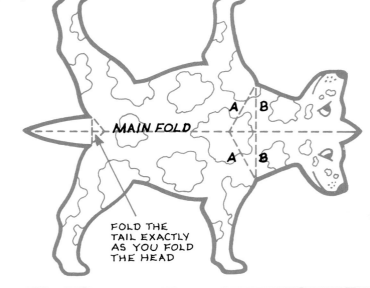

MAIN FOLD

A B

A B

FOLD THE TAIL EXACTLY AS YOU FOLD THE HEAD

1. BEGIN BY DRAWING THE SHAPE OF THE DOG ON TO STIFF PAPER OR CARD. CUT IT OUT, SCORE DOWN THE MAIN FOLD LINE AND FOLD THE DOG IN HALF — PRESS IT FLAT.

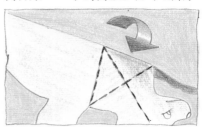

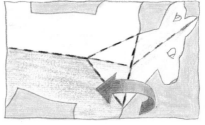

2. OPEN OUT AGAIN AND SCORE THE TWO FOLD LINES MARKED 'A' — FOLD THESE **DOWN.**

3. NEXT SCORE THE TWO LINES MARKED 'B', BUT THIS TIME FOLD THE SCORE LINES **UP.**

4. CLOSE UP THE MAIN FOLD AND PUSH THE FOLDS IN AT THE NECK TO MAKE THE HEAD STAND UP.

5. USING SCISSORS, CUT A SLOT BETWEEN THE EARS.

6. ROLL BOTH OF THE EARS TO MAKE THEM CURL.

7. FINALLY, GLUE THE SIDES OF THE HEAD TOGETHER.

20

MAKING THE RAMP

1. DRAW THE RAMP ON TO STIFF CARD AND CUT IT OUT.

FOLD
FOLD
FOLD

3cm (1¼ in)

FOLD

6cm (2¼ in)

RAMP (CUT 1)

2cm (¾ in)   25cm (10 in)   1cm (⅜ in)   1cm (⅜ in)

3cm (1¼ in)

FOLD
FOLD
FOLD

2. SCORE ALL THE FOLD LINES CAREFULLY AND FOLD UP AS SHOWN ABOVE.

...LET THE GLUE DRY, AND...

3. GLUE ALONG BOTH SIDES AND SQUEEZE THEM TOGETHER...

4. FOLD DOWN THE BACK FLAP AND GLUE THE TABS INSIDE THE SIDES.

IF YOU CAN KNOCK US ALL OVER, YOU WILL WIN THE GAME!

...TURN THE PAGE TO FIND OUT HOW YOU PLAY 'ANIMAL SKITTLES'

21

HOW TO PLAY SKITTLES

First of all, make a base from a spare piece of card. Each square should be drawn large enough for an animal to stand inside it. Number the squares – worth points from 1 to 6 – as shown.

Set up the ramp and position the base. Each player takes turns to roll a marble down the ramp to knock over the animals.

The person who knocks down the most – *and gets the highest score!* – wins the game. Each player should have at least three goes.

HIGHEST SCORE FROM ONE ROLL – 21 POINTS!

Animal Patterns

Now that you know how to make paper animals, here are some others for you to try. You can create your own zoo, or a farm, or even a jungle scene!

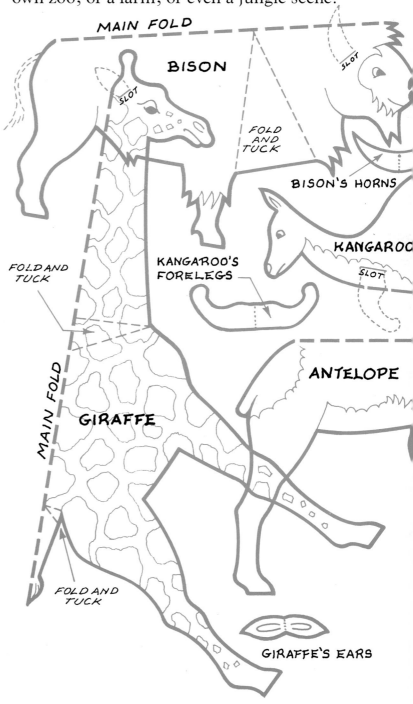

MAIN FOLD

BISON

SLOT

SLOT

FOLD AND TUCK

BISON'S HORNS

KANGAROO'S FORELEGS

KANGAROO

SLOT

FOLD AND TUCK

MAIN FOLD

ANTELOPE

GIRAFFE

FOLD AND TUCK

GIRAFFE'S EARS

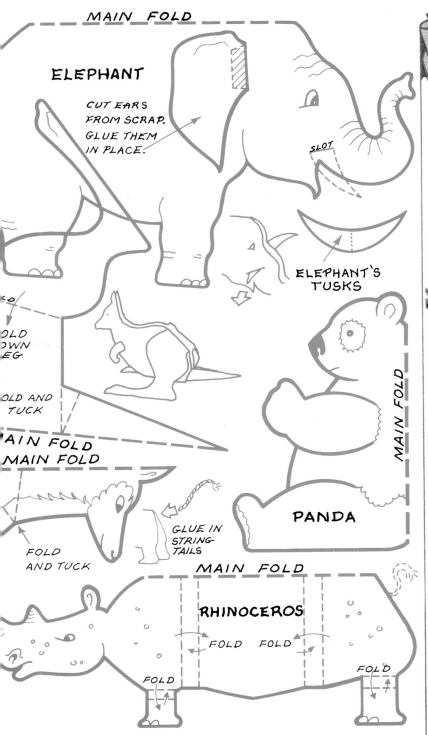

MAIN FOLD

ELEPHANT

CUT EARS FROM SCRAP. GLUE THEM IN PLACE.

SLOT

ELEPHANT'S TUSKS

...O/
...OLD
...OWN
...EG

...OLD AND TUCK

...AIN FOLD
MAIN FOLD

FOLD AND TUCK

GLUE IN STRING TAILS

MAIN FOLD

PANDA

MAIN FOLD

RHINOCEROS

FOLD   FOLD

FOLD

FOLD

ALL OF THESE ANIMALS HAVE BEEN DRAWN AS ONE SIDE ONLY. CUT EACH OF THEM OUT FROM FOLDED PAPER — THE PAPER FOLD SHOULD BE PLACED ALONG THE MAIN FOLD ON THE DRAWING.

PAINTING ANIMALS

To make your animals really life-like, you should colour them in. You can use felt-tip pens or water paints. If you choose paints, don't use too much water or the paper will crinkle.

It's easier to colour your model before you cut it out – if your colour goes over the outer line you can cut it off and it won't show.

Some animals, like the giraffe, have more than one colour. Paint the lightest colour first – then add the darkest.

Don't forget to give your animal an expression.

← HAPPY
SAD →

← SLEEPY
CROSS →

LISTENING
STUPID →

Joker's Wheel ★

This is a great gadget to make – and one that will make all your friends laugh! On the opposite page are lots of jokes, but you can choose your own if you have any favourites!

You will need: 3 pieces of stiff card 20cm × 20cm (8in × 8in); 1 small paper fastener; a pen (to write down your jokes); coloured pens or pencils.

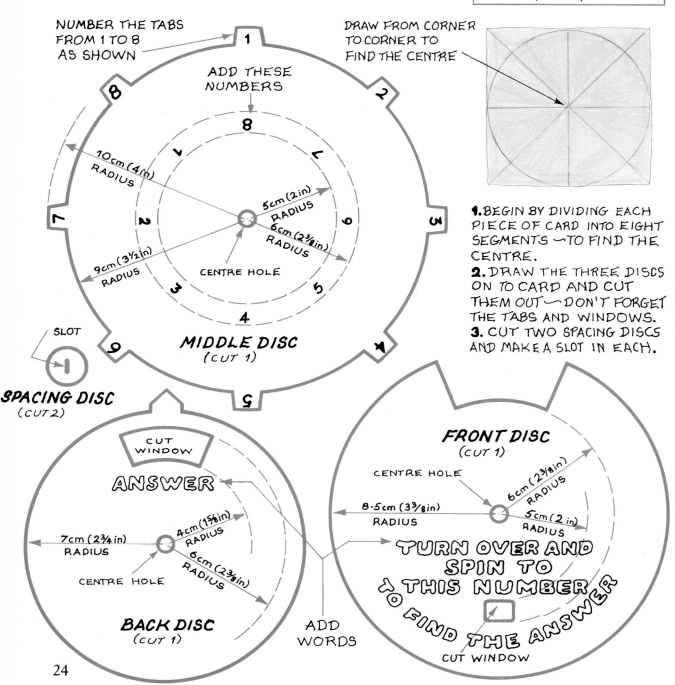

NUMBER THE TABS FROM 1 TO 8 AS SHOWN

DRAW FROM CORNER TO CORNER TO FIND THE CENTRE

ADD THESE NUMBERS

10cm (4in) RADIUS

9cm (3½in) RADIUS

5cm (2in) RADIUS

6cm (2⅜in) RADIUS

CENTRE HOLE

MIDDLE DISC (CUT 1)

1. BEGIN BY DIVIDING EACH PIECE OF CARD INTO EIGHT SEGMENTS ⟶ TO FIND THE CENTRE.
2. DRAW THE THREE DISCS ON TO CARD AND CUT THEM OUT ⟶ DON'T FORGET THE TABS AND WINDOWS.
3. CUT TWO SPACING DISCS AND MAKE A SLOT IN EACH.

SLOT

SPACING DISC (CUT 2)

CUT WINDOW

ANSWER

7cm (2¾in) RADIUS

4cm (1⅝in) RADIUS

6cm (2⅜in) RADIUS

CENTRE HOLE

BACK DISC (CUT 1)

ADD WORDS

FRONT DISC (CUT 1)

CENTRE HOLE

6cm (2⅜in) RADIUS

8.5cm (3⅜in) RADIUS

5cm (2in) RADIUS

TURN OVER AND SPIN TO THIS NUMBER TO FIND THE ANSWER

CUT WINDOW

24

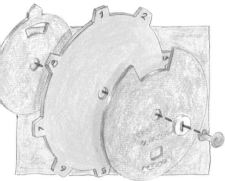

4. FASTEN THE THREE DISCS TOGETHER WITH A PAPER FASTENER. USE A SPACING DISC ON EITHER SIDE.

5. USING THE FRONT DISC AS A GUIDE, WRITE A JOKE QUESTION IN EACH OF THE SEGMENTS — FROM 1 TO 8.

6. NOW NUMBER THE TABS ON THE MIDDLE DISC — **ON THE BACK** — IN ANY ORDER FROM 1 TO 8.

7. FINALLY, USE THE SMALL WINDOW IN THE BACK DISC AS A GUIDE TO WRITE IN THE JOKE ANSWERS.

HERE'S HOW TO DO IT...

Joke 1 shows the number 4 in the small window. Turn the wheel over and spin the back disc until it points to number 4. Write the answer to joke number 1 in the window of the back disc. Repeat all the way round for all the numbers until complete.

JOKES

Q. What do you get if you cross an elephant with a fish?
A. **Swimming trunks!**

Q. What do you call an angry gorilla?
A. **Sir!**

Q. What goes 'Ha, Ha, Ha,...thud!'?
A. **A man laughing his head off!**

Q. What would you give to a sick bird?
A. **First aid tweetment!**

Q. Where do policemen live?
A. **Letsby Avenue!**

Q. How does a pig smell without his nose?
A. **Still pretty awful!**

Q. 'Waiter! What's this fly doing in my soup?'
A. **'Swimming, Sir!'**

Q. Why are elephants extremely wrinkled?
A. **Nobody can iron them!**

Ticking Clock

This model will really amaze your friends! Not only can you move the hands of the clock to alter the time, but when you set the pendulum swinging – it ticks! Look at the drawings carefully to see how it works – it's really very simple.

You will need: 1 piece of stiff card 20cm × 20cm (8in × 8in); 1 piece of stiff card 20cm × 15cm (8in × 6in); 1 wooden matchbox; 2 wooden matchsticks; 1 paper fastener; 1 medium-sized paper clip; cotton thread; a weight (plasticene is just right for this); and some glue.

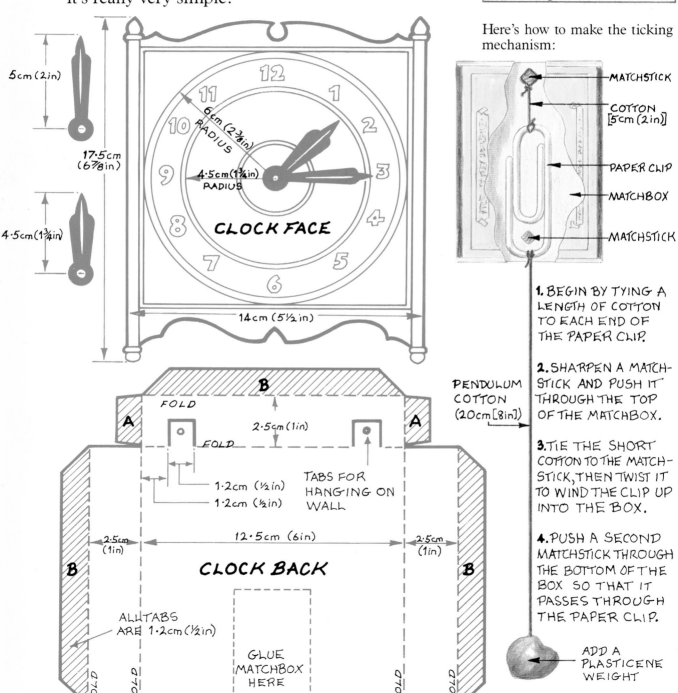

5cm (2in)

17.5cm (6⅞in)

4.5cm (1¾in)

6cm (2⅜in) RADIUS

4.5cm (1¾in) RADIUS

CLOCK FACE

14cm (5½in)

Here's how to make the ticking mechanism:

MATCHSTICK

COTTON [5cm (2in)]

PAPER CLIP

MATCHBOX

MATCHSTICK

1. BEGIN BY TYING A LENGTH OF COTTON TO EACH END OF THE PAPER CLIP.

2. SHARPEN A MATCHSTICK AND PUSH IT THROUGH THE TOP OF THE MATCHBOX.

3. TIE THE SHORT COTTON TO THE MATCHSTICK, THEN TWIST IT TO WIND THE CLIP UP INTO THE BOX.

4. PUSH A SECOND MATCHSTICK THROUGH THE BOTTOM OF THE BOX SO THAT IT PASSES THROUGH THE PAPER CLIP.

PENDULUM COTTON (20cm [8in])

ADD A PLASTICENE WEIGHT

Clock Back

FOLD

B

A

A

FOLD

2.5cm (1in)

1.2cm (½in)

1.2cm (½in)

TABS FOR HANGING ON WALL

2.5cm (1in)

12.5cm (6in)

2.5cm (1in)

B

B

CLOCK BACK

ALL TABS ARE 1.2cm (½in)

GLUE MATCHBOX HERE

FOLD   FOLD   FOLD   FOLD

5. GLUE THE MATCHSTICKS IN PLACE AND CUT OFF THE ENDS.

7. GLUE THE MATCHBOX MECHANISM INTO THE BACK

9. CUT OUT BOTH THE HANDS AND FIT WITH A PAPER FASTENER.

6. USE THE LARGEST PIECE OF CARD FOR THE CLOCK BACK. CUT IT OUT, SCORE AND FOLD, AND GLUE IN THE TWO TABS MARKED 'A'.

8. DRAW THE CLOCK FACE ON TO THE SMALLER CARD. CUT IT OUT AND COLOUR IN ALL THE DETAILS — ADD THE NUMBERS ALL ROUND.

10. FINALLY, APPLY GLUE TO THE TABS MARKED 'B' ON THE CLOCK BACK AND STICK IT TO THE FACE. **...SWING THE PENDULUM!**

27

Penguin Roundabout

This attractive toy is easy to make, but it will only work properly, if the main spindle is made really tight and stiff. You will need to make four penguins, but you can add more if you like; they should be spaced evenly around the roundabout platform.

You will need: 1 piece of stiff card 18cm × 18cm (7in × 7in) – for the platform and the base; 1 piece of stiff paper 23cm × 12cm (9in × 4½in) – for the spindle; 1 piece of stiff paper 20cm × 20cm (8in × 8in) – for the cap and the penguins; cotton thread; and some glue.

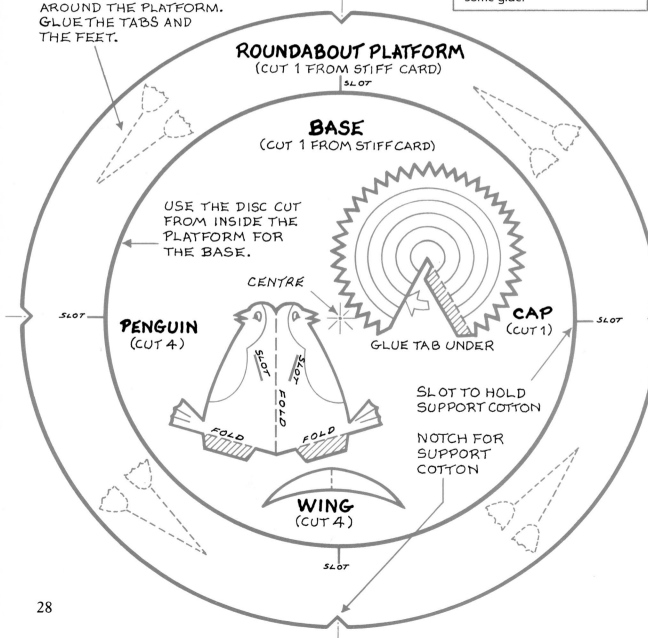

POSITION THE 4 PENGUINS AROUND THE PLATFORM. GLUE THE TABS AND THE FEET.

ROUNDABOUT PLATFORM
(CUT 1 FROM STIFF CARD)

SLOT

BASE
(CUT 1 FROM STIFF CARD)

USE THE DISC CUT FROM INSIDE THE PLATFORM FOR THE BASE.

CENTRE

CAP
(CUT 1)

GLUE TAB UNDER

PENGUIN
(CUT 4)

SLOT

SLOT
FOLD
SLOT
FOLD
FOLD

SLOT

SLOT TO HOLD SUPPORT COTTON

NOTCH FOR SUPPORT COTTON

WING
(CUT 4)

SLOT

STIFF PAPER

SPINDLE TOP

GLUE

SPINDLE CAP

SUPPORT THREADS

SPINDLE BASE

PLATFORM

1. ROLL UP THE STIFF PAPER FOR THE SPINDLE, MAKING A TIGHT TUBE — APPLY GLUE AS YOU ROLL IT UP.

2. CUT 4 NOTCHES IN THE SPINDLE TOP FOR THE SUPPORT THREADS.

3. THE SUPPORT THREADS GO OVER THE TOP NOTCHES, UNDER THE PLATFORM, UP THROUGH THE MIDDLE AND INTO THE SLOTS.

4. CUT 4 SLOTS 3 cm (1¼ in) IN THE FOOT OF THE SPINDLE, FOLD THEM OUT AND THEN GLUE THEM TO THE BASE.

5. MAKE UP THE CAP AND GLUE IT ON TOP OF THE SPINDLE.

MAKING THE PENGUIN

1. CUT OUT AND FOLD DOWN THE BACK.

2. CUT OUT THE WING AND PUSH THROUGH THE SLOTS.

3. TWIST THE FEET FLAT SO THAT YOU CAN GLUE THEM TO THE PLATFORM.

29

Christmas Mobile

Although this mobile is made specially for Christmas, you can use the same method to make a mobile for any occasion. Instead of angels you can make lanterns, animals or even aeroplanes.

You will need: 2 garden sticks 15cm (6in) long; 1 garden stick 30cm (12in) long; strong cotton thread; scraps of stiff paper for the tiny angels; and some glue.

MAKING AN ANGEL

First of all, cut out enough pieces to make 6 angels. Fold along all the fold lines.

1. ROLL THE BODY INTO A CONE SHAPE AND GLUE THE TAB MARKED 'A' RIGHT DOWN THE BACK INSIDE THE CONE.

2. FOLD UP THE FEET.

3. GLUE THE ARMS TO THE FRONT OF THE BODY AND THE WINGS TO THE BACK. GLUE THE HANDS TOGETHER.

4. FOLD OUT THE HALO AT EACH SIDE, THEN CLOSE UP THE HEAD AND GLUE BOTH THE HEAD SHAPES TOGETHER.

5. GLUE THE ENDS OF THE HALO TOGETHER AT 'B' AND GLUE THE COMPLETED HEAD INTO THE TOP OF THE CONE.

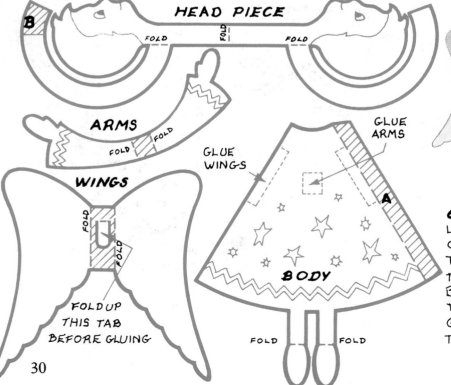

HEAD PIECE

FOLD   FOLD   FOLD

B

ARMS

FOLD   FOLD

WINGS

FOLD   FOLD

FOLD UP THIS TAB BEFORE GLUING

GLUE WINGS

GLUE ARMS

A

BODY

FOLD   FOLD

6. FINALLY, TIE A LONG LENGTH OF COTTON THREAD TO THE TAB BETWEEN THE WINGS. GLUE DOWN THE TAB TO THE BODY.

30